PEACE PLAN

VANISH STRESS BY USING SIMPLE TECHNIQUES

UDAYASREE REDDY

Made with ♥ on the Notion Press Platform
www.notionpress.com

Contents

About The Author

Udayasree Reddy, a 2nd year UG student in the field of psychology, a 18- year - old. She is interested in counseling psychology.

Encouraged by her parents Prameela and Raghunath Reddy to choose her own career path, she stands out here explaining how to vanish stress in every day life. By looking at the people how stressed they are in this era of living.

Review

Dr G Saravana Kumar, Professor

CMR University, BENGALURU

DHMCT, BA(Eco), MBA(T&HM),NET(T), PhD

The book titled, "PEACE PLAN" written by author Udaya Reddy, deals with a contemporary topic of stress and depression which is faced by many working people and also students in present days and hence it is a significant topic. Author has explained the various causes for stress and depression with case studies in 3 chapters, which is simple and understandable by all. The health-related problems caused to people due to prolonged stress and also due to habits like smoking and drinking has been explained scientifically. The author has also clarified in detail the difference between stress and depression and its connections in Chapter 2. She has made a good suggestion of Cognitive behavioural therapy (CBT) to overcome stress. In Chapter 3 author has dealt in detail about how to overcome stress which has valuable suggestions like breathing exercises and meditation technique, which is really going to benefit the readers to come out of stress. Being a student of Psychology Author Udaya has discussed about the problem of stress from various points of view like students, working people etc.

Over all the book has been written with exhaustive research and references and hence I believe this book will be a valuable and useful resource for working couples, students and also housewives. I appreciate and convey my best wishes to author Ms. Udaya Reddy for bringing this quality book for a good purpose for the common people to live a stress free happy life.

Dr G Saravana Kumar

About The Reviewer

Dr G Saravana Kumar is presently working as a Professor in CMR University, Bengaluru. He has around 22 years of Industry experience in Tourism and hospitality sector and he has rich academic experience fs 13 years. He has worked in reputed Universities as professor and contributed to mentoring many students.

He has done extensive research and has published around 52 research papers in various reputed International and Indian Journals which has received good citations around the globe. He has also authored two books on customer relationship Management and marketing management. He has also guided PhD scholars and still continuing his research guidance. He is in the review & editorial board of two International, Scopus indexed Journals. He has reviewed several research articles for reputed journals.

Review

This is an excellent article defining stress and how to overcome stress in work places as well as daily life of people. In industry people tend to forget their health condition out of work pressure and continue to put more pressure on brain without giving enough cooling time. This article gives insight to people how stress induced in humans can affect their health and how to overcome stress at work place and daily life. The focus on effective stress management on day to day basis defined in this article is excellent and following such steps will help in comfort in living and long life of human beings.

K V Bhaskara Reddy
Former Director (Production & Projects)
KIOCL Limited

Review

Very objectively written case. Different scenarios were examined and explained. Substance abuse due to stress leads to altered mental mechanisms.

Dr. Sai Kiran

ONE
Introduction of Stress

———❦———

You will learn about the person's behavior during stressful times as you read this chapter, and you will also learn about a way to deal with stress.

Abstract: Stress is a complicated, multidimensional phenomenon that influences how people react to difficult situations by making them feel tense both physically and emotionally. Basically, stress is the body's reaction to perceived dangers or difficulties. It sets off a series of physiological events that include the release of cortisol and adrenaline. Although these reactions are beneficial in the short term, using them over an extended period of time may be harmful to one`s health.

Long-term stress has a detrimental effect on relationships and productivity at work, which can lead to a vicious cycle of unfavorable interactions and reduced output. Chronic stress has also been connected to a host of other health issues, including as anxiety, depression, weakened immune systems, and cardiovascular disease.

Additionally, stress has an impact on cognitive processes, which can result in issues with focus, memory, and judgment. Lastly, stress can result in issues with mindfulness, exercise, and social support.

Introduction: These days, stress permeates every aspect of our life and affects people of all ages, social classes, and cultural orientations. Stress can be brought on by a variety of factors, including personal struggles, societal obligations, and responsibilities to one's family and job. Although stress is a normal reaction that helps us get through challenging times, too much or too little of it can be harmful to our general well-being, physical and mental health, and standard of living.This version will address the basic concepts of stress as well as its sources, effects, and practical management and reduction techniques. We might better equip ourselves with the information and resources necessary to lead healthier, more resilient lives if we are more aware of the effects of stress.

We will examine how our bodies and minds react to stressful situations as we investigate the physiological and psychological components of stress in this research. We'll also look at the different sources of stress, which include both internal and external factors like perfectionism and negative thought patterns, as well as external stressors like deadlines and financial strain.

We'll also look at the myriad detrimental impacts that stress has on our well-being, such as how it can lead to the onset of long-term conditions like dysregulated immune systems, heart problems, and mental health issues like anxiety and depression. Understanding the detrimental effects stress has on our physical and emotional well-being can help us prioritize self-care and take proactive steps to lower our stress levels.

Lastly, we will go over stress-reduction strategies that research has proven to be effective, such as social support networks, physical activity, mindfulness, and relaxation. We may strengthen our coping skills, increase our resilience, and foster a better feeling of balance and wellness by implementing these techniques into our daily lives.

Let's acknowledge the value of empathy, self-awareness, and self-care as we begin this exploration of the intricate phenomenon of stress. Through acquiring knowledge and adopting proactive measures to manage stress, we might potentially become more adept at handling life's challenges with ease and resilience.

Stress-producing elements:

Stress can manifest itself in a variety of ways for the current generation, such as:

1. **Academic Pressure:** Students frequently face stress due to their academic achievement, exams, and expectations from parents and teachers in an increasingly competitive educational environment.
2. **Technological Overload:** Although technology has many advantages, there are drawbacks as well. Being always connected can cause stress because of FOMO, information overload, and social media pressure.

3. **Financial Stress**: Exorbitant living expenses, debt from school loans, and unpredictability in the economy can all lead to stress, especially for young individuals just beginning their careers.
4. **Career-Related Concerns**: Tough work situations, employment insecurity, and the need to achieve professionally can all considerably increase stress levels.
5. **Social Pressures**: Social media has contributed to the rise of social comparison, which eases the pressure to manage relationships, fit in, and have sex.
6. **Family dynamics**: Stress can be caused by parent expectations, family conflicts, and obligations to younger siblings or aging parents.
7. **Mental Health difficulties**: It's being increasingly widely acknowledged that social stigma, a lack of access to mental health care, and the pressure to appear "perfect" on social media exacerbate depression, anxiety, and other mental health difficulties.
8. **Environmental Concerns**: Young individuals who worry about the future of the earth can occasionally experience existential stress and Eco-anxiety due to climate change, natural disasters, and environmental degradation.

The mental, emotional, and physical well-being of people in the current generation can be significantly impacted by these pressures, among other things. To increase resilience and wellness, it is essential to address these problems through selfcare practices, support networks, and societal reforms.

Let's now look at how people live their lives and react to stress.

Story 1: Stressful every day says ARUVI,

Aruvi was employed by the Hyderabad-based IT sector. She was married to Kishore, an IT worker as well. Four years have passed since their marriage. After a few days of marriage, she began to experience stress from the pressures of their jobs at the office, which also caused relationship problems in their personal lives. Now, let's see what disruptions she is experiencing.

She was not happy with the amount of labor she was paid since she worked too much and was unable to communicate openly about her problems at work. She has work-related stress every five to six days. Because her spouse works night shifts and she works day shifts in their offices, she was also dissatisfied and stressed about their intimate relationship. Their private lives are being negatively impacted by their inability to enjoy their sexual relationship because of their long work hours and out-of-town travels. She seldom has two days off a week for leisure. She has to manage her office job, caring for her infant, and household chores, all in addition to working twelve to fifteen hours a day. She has been enduring stress for the past two years because it's difficult to handle everything as a parent. She is attempting to balance her work and obligations critically. She works in a position where there are many stressful components, such as teamwork and communication, technical changes, and tight deadlines. She probably won't recommend a position in her organization to anyone who isn't a bachelor. When she gets too anxious, she attempts to go to some psychologists for treatment sessions or indulge in her hobbies, like gardening, etc. Even if she finds it difficult to talk to her employer about stress-related issues, she makes an effort to be close to him by planning ahead, setting up a meeting, outlining the consequences, speaking in a calm and clear manner, etc. She has to deal with bad work habits such as a long-term sedentary lifestyle, erratic sleep schedules, and inadequate nutrition and diet. She advises making a solid timetable and adhering to it in order to improve work-life balance and avoid overthinking any one task. Additionally, Aruvi said that there are advantages and disadvantages to working remotely, like fewer commutes, environmental control, isolation, frequent check-ins, technical difficulties, etc. The impact of team dynamics, including leadership, communication, cooperation, support, and dispute resolution, also significantly contributes to stress.

They had troubles in their relationship occasionally, which stressed her out to the point where she lost tolerance and began lashing out at little things that they would normally brush off. This could lead to excessive reactions. She began to isolate herself in a room and avoid social interactions with friends and relatives. She also has raw rice and slate pencils in order to reduce her stress. She should be aware of many indicators in their relationships, such as heightened irritability and short temper, mood swings, and avoidance of social situations, which suggest their stress may be impacting others. To discuss her concern with loved ones without causing strife, she must pick the appropriate moment and location, gently express her feelings, be open and honest, and consider other viewpoints. She can establish and maintain healthy boundaries by putting in place a number of strategies, such as clearly defining work hours and refraining from working beyond those times, designating a specific area for workspace to prevent blurring lines, responding to a limited number of messages, and turning off notifications to prevent interruptions. This will help to ensure that their stress doesn't overwhelm their relationships. She added that their loved ones encourage her and help her with chores when she is under stress. She also asked for assistance in starting a conversation to share how they are feeling in order to feel less stressed, and she also expressed gratitude for their support.

Intimate relationships, she added, can have a big impact on IT workers' stress levels. They can either increase or decrease it because of emotional strain caused by things like frequent arguments, a lack of support, or emotional disconnection. Personal conflicts can also affect work life, making it harder for an individual to focus and perform well, as well as adding additional responsibilities. She also shared several strategies from her experience for reducing stress, including unwinding and having fun in the form of A meaningful break from the stress of work can be obtained by spending time with a significant other. She can decompress and rejuvenate by relaxing, pursuing hobbies, or participating in recreational activities with their partner. Perspective and encouragement Partners can provide an alternative viewpoint on work-related matters, assisting their professionals in gaining understanding and potentially resolving obstacles. Partner encouragement can raise spirits and confidence, which makes taking on challenges at work simpler. Stress Mitigation Strategies Creating and sustaining good stress management practices can be assisted by partners and can involve promoting mindfulness exercises, a balanced diet, enough sleep, and frequent exercise. Maintaining these practices even during times of severe work stress might be aided by a supportive partner.In order to properly handle stress in their relationship, she strikes a balance between their personal space and their closeness. She employs strategies like Plan specified times for work and personal activities and have regular conversations with partners and family members about work schedules, stress levels, and personal needs. Setting aside time each day for work and relationships by using tools like calendars and reminders.

Additionally, their friends had a greater impact on her stress levels in a variety of ways. She shared her concerns and received validation for them, and her peers gave her more confidence and moral support. The strain that her coworkers' loved ones endure can have a big effect on the employees themselves. She explained that a number of mechanisms, including relational tension, increasing obligations, and emotional contagion, cause this occurrence. Maintaining healthy relationships and overall well-being requires an understanding of and the ability to manage this interrelated stress.She also offered a few tactics. When a relationship itself starts to become stressful, engage in active listening techniques by paying close attention to what your partner is saying, demonstrating empathy, and giving meaningful, non-interruption responses. You can also consider seeking pair therapy from a psychologist. She suggested a few ways to manage this situation by noticing their spike in anxiety or stress without a clear personal cause, by absorbing the stress of others, and by taking practical steps like using regular breaks as well as creating a dedicated workspace. Recognize signs that she might be taking on the stress of others and establish healthy emotional boundaries. She defuses tense situations in relationships by observing nonverbal signs, identifying triggers, and demonstrating empathy. She also strengthens her resilience in their relationship by recognizing and supporting her loved ones throughout their times of need. Despite her stress, she was able to keep her relationship vibrant and healthy by employing these tactics.

Story 2: A life transitioning from childhood to maturity

A man named Rahul was under pressure and stress because of his academic career. Let's now discuss the challenges he has faced throughout his life began to experience stress as a result of the pressure to perform well academically and manage his time, which came from his parents, instructors, and himself. Delaying duties can cause procrastination, which can result in a last-minute rush and more stress. Social and interpersonal problems with friends and family can also cause stress. His mental health is severely harmed by constant comparison and cyberbully on social media sites. Financial worries and the uncertainty of an unstable future have further increased his strain. When he was under stress, he experienced physical sensations, emotional experiences, behavioral changes, and cognitive repercussions. Throughout the academic year, he experienced daily stress for a variety of reasons, including environmental conditions, health and well-being, and other issues.In addition, he thought that it would be monotonous or difficult to focus in class due to outside distractions or sleep deprivation. Sometimes, because of the instructor's methods and his active participation, or because he is interested in a certain subject, or because there is more discussion on a particular topic, he fully understands what the teacher is teaching him.

He used to miss courses frequently because he was under stress from personal and health difficulties, or occasionally he would experience perceived redundancy. In addition, he feels a great deal of strain from an abundance of homework obligations. Because of his family's financial difficulties and the fact that he is an upper - caste member, he also lacks the funds for his basic necessities. He revealed that he barely makes between $1000 and $1500 a month. Despite living in a wealthy region, he was constantly under pressure from his parents to cut back on his spending, and he was also under pressure from friends to stop making fun of him because of his financial crisis. Along with moving away from home and changing schools, he also experienced loneliness because he had to transfer schools and missed a lot of classes due to health concerns. He felt insecure about his GPA. Because of his poor health and depression, he also lost weight. He used to experience a great deal of stress during his tests due to his improper attendance and inability to cover the entire. Due to remote learning at the time of COVID, he had stress in his academic setting during that period. After his graduation, he got placed in his school. By the time he left school, he suggested higher authorities in school help students with lower stress levels by teaching them relaxation techniques and giving them less homework and assignments.

As a trainee, he was employed by Cap-Gemini and received an average compensation package. His new team put him under a lot of work pressure, and his boss bullied him into finishing the assignment ahead of schedule. His inability to manage his goals and his lack of abilities prevented him from communicating effectively, which made him stressed out from the demands of his job. As he was sitting for long working hours in his office, he was strained from back pain and eye irritation due to the long screening time.He was more stressed because of family problems, like financial issues. His parents spent on his education by borrowing money from moneylenders for debt, and he was unable to pay those in a short period of time because he gets less of a salary, and he loves a girl, and their parents are not accepting their relationship for marriage because the girl was from another caste, and also because he cannot proceed with eloping, so he was depressed.

Due to depression, he started smoking anyway. He got convinced through his parents and married another girl, and he was unable to forget the memories of his first love. He was continuously smoking, and because of that, he got cancer and is undergoing treatment now.

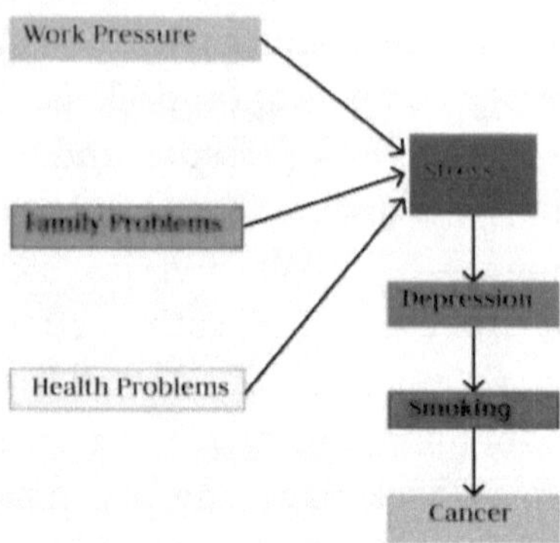

In recent days, what I observed is that most of the bachelors are stressed because their parents are forcing them to get married; they are not showing interest in getting engaged because they are scared to manage family responsibilities with the salaries they get; and most of the IT workers are not sure about their jobs. As they are stressed, they are habituated to consume alcohol, drugs, and smoke. They have forgotten the statement that smoking causes cancer and affects the lungs. As they were continuously smoking, they got affected by cancer, lung diseases, and diabetes, also leads to impotency in their intimate relationships.

[NOTE: Some of the studies say that erectile dysfunction will affect about 332 million men by 2025 due to hypertension].

Imminent high pressure causes increased anger issues, which lead to stress. As soon as they are stressed, they are isolating themselves. Being isolated and disconnected from people for more than 2 weeks leads to depression. As they were depressed, overthinking increased among them, which leads to suicidal thoughts, and most of the young have been ending their lives at a very young age.

[NOTE: Another study says more than 48,000 people died by suicide in - 2021 that is 1 death every 11 minutes. 12.3 adults considered suicide, 3.5 million made a plan for suicide, and 1.7 adults committed suicide].

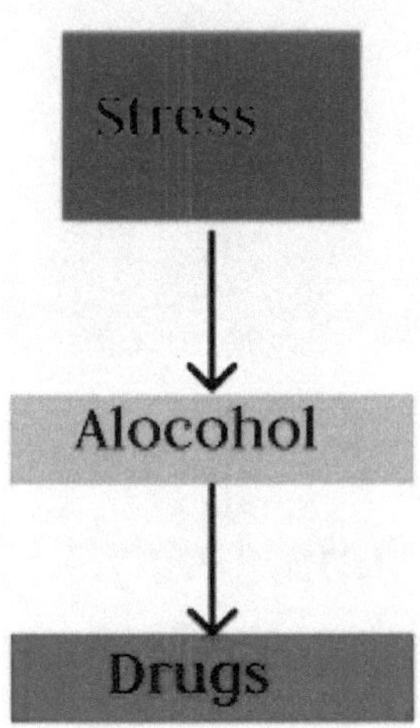

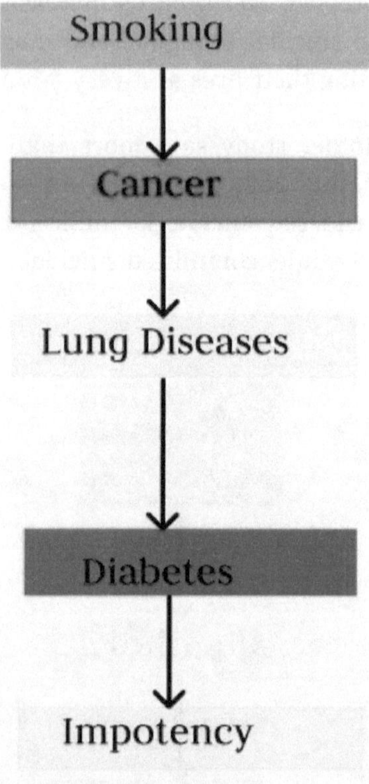

The link between perfectionism and stress:

The traits associated with the perfectionist personality type include high standards for performance, an obsession with perfection, and excessive self- and other-criticism. When perfectionism and outside influences are compared, several important conclusions are drawn

Perfectionism's Stress-Inducing Nature: Self-imposed stress: People who are perfectionists typically put a lot of pressure on themselves to live up to unreasonable expectations, which leads to ongoing tension. The effects of outside pressures might be made worse by this tension that you've put on yourself.

Fear of Failure: Daily struggles might become more difficult for perfectionists who are afraid of making mistakes or hearing negative comments from others.

Enhanced Response to External Stressors:

Overreaction to Criticism: Rather than seeing criticism as helpful advice, perfectionists may become more emotionally charged when faced with it or take offense at it.

Having Trouble Handling Uncertainty: Perfectionists who depend on predictability and control may find it particularly difficult to handle outside pressures that cause uncertainty or unpredictability.

Relationships with Different Stressors:

Work-related Stress: Due to their high standards, propensity for working long hours, and inability to delegate, perfectionists frequently experience stress at work.

Societal Stress: Social relationships and interactions can be stressful, particularly for perfectionists who believe they are being watched intently or fall short of societal norms.

Effects on Health:

The consequences of outside demands can be amplified by perfectionism, making daily obstacles seem more difficult and unpleasant. Comprehending this connection and applying useful coping strategies might aid perfectionists in stress management and enhance their general well-being.

How can one determine whether they are stressed?

Given that everyone experiences stress differently, it can be challenging to identify. Nonetheless, there are typical indicators and manifestations to be aware of, which can be categorized as behavioral, emotional, mental, or physical.

Indications and symptoms of the body:

Headaches: Recurrent or frequent headaches could indicate stress.

Pain or strain in the muscles: Stress, particularly in the neck, shoulders, and back, is a major cause of muscular strain.

Digestive Disorders: Stress can lead to stomachaches, nausea, and other digestive issues.

Modifications to Sleep Patterns: inability to fall asleep, trouble staying asleep, or excessive sleep.

Indices of feeling: Experiencing unusually high amounts of anger, annoyance, or impatience are signs of feeling.

Anxiety: An ongoing sensation of uneasiness, discomfort, or panic is called anxiety.

Depression: depressing, oppressive, or dismal feelings.

Mood swings: This is sudden, dramatic shifts in feeling.

Mental Indications and Signs:

Trouble Focusing: The inability to maintain concentration or attention. Memory issues include things like forgetting essential information or having difficulty recalling it.

Negative Thinking: An attitude that is consistently depressing or negative. Deciding nothing at all, especially on little matters, is called indecision.

Action marks: shifts in appetite, like eating too much or too little. The procrastination is the act of delaying or avoiding work. The act of removing oneself from friends, family, or activities you typically find delightful is known as social withdrawal.

High substance use: use of cigarettes, alcohol, or drugs as a comfort.

In summary, knowing the phenomenon of stress is necessary to control its impacts on one's physical and mental health. This chapter has addressed the definitions, causes, and effects of stress as well as how it impacts various aspects of life. People can decrease the harmful effects of stress by implementing helpful coping methods if they are aware of its symptoms and causes. Since stress is an inevitable part of life, maintaining overall wellness requires developing resilience and utilizing stress-reduction techniques. Going forward,a more thorough analysis of these techniques and how they are used in everyday life will offer a comprehensive method for managing stress in a healthy way.

TWO
STRESS VS DEPRESSION

As we studied stress levels in a variety of individuals according to their causes, we found that stress can also contribute to depression. Overthinking for longer than two weeks can result in depression, which can then cause stress and vice versa. Based on my investigation, I've found that the majority of IT professionals choose [Swedish SPA] to reduce stress levels brought on by work pressure. Due to the responsibilities and uncertainties of beginning and operating a business, entrepreneurs frequently have unique pressures. They may find it difficult to balance their work, fail to meet targets, or unable to pay employees' salaries.

Stress most often evokes unfavorable feelings in your memory. However, some stress is healthy for you; for example, the excitement you get before beginning a new career or relationship. It can pique your interest and motivate you to take on and accomplish more. Stress can also make you more resilient and ready to handle risky circumstances. Good tension is short-lived. It makes you feel more upbeat for the moment and then fades. Extended duration of stress can be debilitating and have an impact on your physical and mental health.

When our pressure reaction starts in a short amount of time, we perform objectively well; when it starts in a longer amount of time, we perform less well.

THE CONNECTION BETWEEN STRESS & DEPRESSION:

"When we experience prolonged periods of stress, our body's stress response is overworked and begins to malfunction."

Chronic, long-term stress can be harmful to one's health in and of itself, but it can also make depression worse. Depression is a mental condition that makes you feel down and uninterested in things you usually find enjoyable. Depression might affect your eating, sleeping, and attention habits.

In addition, the effects of depression may lead to stress.

"One of the most significant issues of our time is the connection in between stress and depression, and vice versa."

The reverse is likewise strongly suggested by the evidence.

A significant source of stress, is in finances or a divorce, for example, could upset someone's emotional equilibrium. An increase in stress will eventually lead to something, and sadness is frequently the outcome. Less evident are the ways in which stress fuels depression, though.

We assume that increased levels of sadness were caused by social exclusion, skipping out on routine activities, and general stress from job or school disturbances. I would contend, nevertheless, that the exact causative mechanism underlying that is unknown.

GET ASSISTANCE:

Avoiding attempting to manage stress and melancholy on your own is another strategy to lessen their effects. Having solid, encouraging relationships can have a significant impact.

Speaking with friends and family can help you gain a better understanding of the causes of your stress, which will help you make considerable improvement. A state of disconnection is depression. Finding a means of connection would therefore be among the most crucial things. Incorporating a few acquaintances from your past and establishing a connection is crucial

It is advantageous, for example, if someone enquire about your stress management techniques and tell me about your current state of mind together with "How's your tenor?" Then just be mindful.

People can frequently talk to others who listen to them and receive better counsel or solutions to their issues. Ask them open-minded questions without holding back, and pay close attention to the response they provide.

If depression and stress are compounding each other, it might be helpful to identify the specific stressors in your life that are causing the most harm.We're all prone to declare, "I'm stressed," but distinguish the exact problems that are troubling you might be quite helpful.

If you have fears that prevent you from communicating to your family, you can talk to psychologists instead of your relatives. Getting cognitive-behavioral therapy is single strategy to convert your aspect and proceed towards(CBT).

We need to restore control, which is why cognitive behavior therapy is foremost significant.CBT improve you to concentrate on the tiny work you can finish today, as well as how to carry and estimate it. It is therefore an excellent learning and healing creature.

Reference:

Neutral: pressure is a period that has turned to parlance with the current entity. This analysis aims to evaluate the verification connecting stress with disorder with a specific review to the crucial of bitterness and humanity in the western civilization, cardio-respiratory, tumour, and dejection.

Method: A Med-line search was carried out for the period 1996-2000 to identify recent findings in this field using the terms "stress", "disease", "immune system". Investigation was another related source that was established in every determination announcement.

Results:

Research indicates a negative prognosis for cancer and cardiovascular illness, as well as a relationship between stress and the beginning of serious depression. A few tiny studies imply that stress-reduction techniques could enhance survival. While immunological activation and suppression have been linked to acute stress, chronic stress seems to lead to immune response suppression.Depression symptoms may be brought on by soluble immune response mediators called inflammatory cytokines.

Termination:

Additional intended epidemiological studies are required to elucidate the impact of stress on the start, progression, and prognosis of disease. Exciting new research is being done on stress management techniques with the goal of extending survival in people with cancer, cardiovascular disease, and maybe other chronic conditions. Stress and disease may be related due to modifications in the immune system. The "depression, stress, cytokines" hypothesis is our suggested biological explanation for the connection in between depressive symptoms and demanding entity involvement.

THREE
HOW TO OVER COME STRESS

Furthermore,as everyone—children and adults alike experiences stress due to their classified employment, there are strategies to help manage it. We can quickly return to normalcy and experience stress alleviation by using these approaches. I've heard that in order to see results or become accustomed to a schedule, whatever we do should be practiced for a minimum of 21 days.

Let's now study a few techniques/methods to reduce stress ultimately;

Mindfulness and Meditation : Techniques such as mindfulness and meditation have the potential to reduce stress, enhance concentration, and enhance overall health. Use these thorough methods to start and maintain a mindfulness and meditation practice:

Step1: Depending on the availability of time you have, choose a quiet place where you won't be disturbed and set aside at least 10 to 45 minutes each day for practice. You can complete it in the morning or in the evening.

Step 2: Take a seat on the floor, in a chair, or on a cushion, keeping your back straight. You can rest it on your lap or set it on your knee while keeping the Gyan mudra in place.

Step 3: Softly close your eyes when it's comfortable. After that, relax by taking a few deep breaths. Let your breathing to return to its regular rhythm at last. Observe the sensation of breath coming in and going out of your nostrils, the rise and fall of your chest and abdomen.

Step 4: Be attentive to the present moment. Make a note of any sounds, aroma, or physical feelings. If your mind wanders, bring it back to the breath in a calm and slow manner.

Step 5: Start with your toes and work your path up to your head as you gradually shift your concentration from your breath to different body parts. Observe any discomfort, tenseness, or other emotions. Simply note without attempting to change things.

Step 6: Stay open to any thoughts, emotions, or involvements of that surface. Acknowledge them without accepting to ignore or engage with them. Come back to your concentration to the present moment.

Step 7: When it's time to wrap up, gradually pay attention back to the room. Open your eyes and tackle your feelings for a moment before carrying on with your day.

Benefits:lower stress, anxiety, and depression; improve relationships; improve memory; improve cognitive function; improve physical health;

NOTE: Because it is based on a universal human capacity, anyone can practice it.

Breathing Techniques: Breathing exercises are ways to improve overall well being, reduce stress, sharpen focus, and increase respiratory health. Here are several popular and practical breathing techniques:

Belly breathing or diaphragmatic breathing: This technique involves contracting the diaphragm in order to fully fill the lungs with air.

Select a comfortable sitting or lying position. Put a palm on your chest and one on your stomach Inhale deeply through your nose, allowing your chest to stay mostly still and your stomach to rise. As you gradually release the breath through your mouth, feel your stomach drop. For five to 10 minutes, keep going.

Benefits:include lowered heart rate and blood pressure, a stronger diaphragm, reduced anxiety, a reduction in the amount of energy and effort needed to breathe, better COPD (chronic obstructive pulmonary disease) symptoms, and a decrease in asthma symptoms.

NOTE: When practicing belly breathing, those with respiratory disorders like COPD or asthma should use caution.

Box breathing or square breathing: It is a method that Navy seals and athletes regularly utilize to maintain composure and concentrate.

Inhale for four counts via your nose.

Hold your breath for four counts.

For four counts, exhale through your mouth.

Hold your breath for four counts.

Repeat the cycle several times.

Benefits: Include lowering bodily stress, improving mental clarity, vitality, and attention, strengthening future stressreaction mechanisms, improving sleep, promoting pleasant emotions and mental states, improving mood, stimulating the parasympathetic nervous system, and helping to manage anxiety and tension when feeling overburdened.

NOTE: Because box breathing necessitates holding the breath, it might not be suitable for people who struggle with it. Those who have high blood pressure or who are pregnant should see a doctor before trying it.

4-7-8 Breathing: This technique, often known as the calming breath, is meant to reduce stress and encourage calmness.

Sit or lie down comfortably.

After closing your eyes, inhale four slow breaths through your nose.

Hold your breath for seven counts.

Breathe out through your mouth completely for eight counts.

Go through steps 4-6 several times.

Benefits: include calming your nervous system and intellect, reducing emotional reactions like rage, controlling food cravings, lowering stress and anxiety levels, improving the quality of your sleep, raising awareness and focus, regulating the body's response to fight or flight, and facilitating a faster fall asleep.

NOTE: This technique is fairly safe and can significantly enhance your health. However, until you get more used to the workout, you should only complete four cycles at a time at first. Breath work should not be done if you are pregnant or suffer from a significant medical condition.

Alternate Nostril Inhalation (Nadi Shodhana): This yoga breathing technique is said to balance the left and right hemispheres of the brain.

Sitting comfortably requires maintaining a straight back.Breathe deeply through your left nostril while closing your right nostril with your thumb. Close your left nostril with your right ring finger, then open your right nostril and breathe through it. Inhale deeply via your right nostril. Shut your right nostril once more and exhale through your left. For a few minutes, keep doing this.

Benefits:include reducing stress and anxiety, calming the body and mind, strengthening lung and respiratory function by harmonizing the brain's hemispheres and the neurological system, raising awareness and focus, preparing oneself mentally for meditation.

NOTE: You may wish to stop practice if you have a fever, a seizure disorder, or a severe headache. Those with high blood pressure, asthma, or any other lung or heart issues should consult a physician before implementing this practice into their regular regimen.

Resonant Breathing (Coherent Breathing): This method uses five breaths per minute to reduce stress and increase heart rate variability.

Take a five-second breath.

Let out a five-second breath.

Repeat for ten minutes or more.

Benefits: include pain alleviation, better sleep quality, heightened vitality and energy, mindfulness, and awareness of the here and now.

NOTE: Avoid the practice if you're feeling under the weather or sick.

Pursed Lip Breathing: This breathing method helps to slow down breathing and is commonly used by people with lung diseases.

Breathe slowly through your nose for two counts.

Hold your lips in the form of blowing air and exhale.

Pursed lips should emit four steady, soft breaths.Repeat many times.

Benefits: improving ventilation by letting new, fresh oxygen enter the lungs and replacing old air (carbon dioxide) that has been trapped there; lowering the rate at which one breathes and keeping the airways open for a longer period of time to relieve shortness of breath.

NOTE: People with severe chest injuries, respiratory illnesses, or vertigo should not perform this exercise.

Exercise as a stress-relieving strategy:

Aerobic exercises: These are a kind of rhythmic, repetitive exercise that target the major muscle groups in your body.

For instance, brisk cycling, swimming, walking, and running.

Benefits: include improved heart health, happier mood, and the production of feel-good hormones.

Strength training: This involves using your muscles to resist external forces.

Benefits: include boosted self-esteem, reduced stress, and strengthened and stretched muscles.

Yoga: This physical, mental, and spiritual discipline originated in ancient India. The sage Patanjali first codified it in his Yoga Sutra, circa 400 CE.

Benefits: Promotes flexibility and relaxation by combining deep breathing, meditation, and physical activity.

Outdoor Activities: It is experienced when working out physically.

For instance: kayaking, hiking, and gardening.

Benefits:exposing individuals to outdoors has been shown to reduce stress and improve mood.

Dance: This type of performance art involves arranging events in a certain order.

Benefits: Boosts heart rate, improves social interaction, and is intriguing and amusing.

Nutrition under stress:

Stress can have a significant effect on general health and nutrition. An individual's eating habits, nutritional status, and nutrient absorption can all be impacted by the physiological changes that stress causes in the body. Considering the relationship between stress and diet, bear the following in mind:

When people are under stress, their eating habits can change. For example, emotional eating can result in overindulging in high-fat, high-calorie, and high-sugar foods. It also serves as a coping strategy for unpleasant feelings.Few people, however, may experience food reduction, loss of appetite, and other nutritional inadequacies when under stress.

Furthermore, long-term stress can deplete the body of essential minerals like magnesium, vitamin C, and B vitamins, all of which are necessary for stress management and the upkeep of a healthy neurological system. Possible side effects of chronic stress include elevated blood sugar levels and an increase in appetites for fatty and sugary meals due to the generation of cortisol.Additionally, because digestive disorders can impact nutrition absorption and general gut health, they can worsen gastrointestinal conditions, including acid reflex, irritable bowel syndrome (IBS), and other gastrointestinal disorders.

Sometimes,stress can impact on metabolism, causing either weight gain or reduction. Elevated cortisol levels have been linked to fat storage, especially in the abdominal region

Few Healthy Eating Techniques to Reduce Stress:

Maintaining a diet high in whole grains, fruits, vegetables, lean meats, and healthy fats will help maintain a stable mood and energy level.Some complicated sugars like whole grains and other foods can raise serotonin levels, which are a neurotransmitter that aids in mood regulation and also keeping hydrated is important for one's general health and can support sustained energy and focus. By practicing mindful eating, people can become more conscious of their eating habits and make healthier food choices. It also increases personal fulfillment and pleasure and also regularly eating wellbalanced meals will help maintain the body healthy and fit, reduce stress-induced cravings, and help control blood sugar levels.

Dietary Supplements for Stress Reduction:

Nuts and whole green vegetables are excellent source of magnesium. It aids in nervous system calmness and muscular relaxation. Legumes, leafy greens, eggs, and whole grains all include B vitamins. They are essential to the synthesis of energy and brain activity. Fatty Acids Omega-3 present in walnuts, flax-seeds, and fatty fish. They promote the health of the brain and have anti-inflammatory qualities. Vitamin C Found in bell peppers, strawberries, and citrus fruits. It boosts immunological response and lessens oxidative stress.

People can promote their health and well-being during stressful times by making informed decisions based on their understanding of the relationship between stress and nutrition.

Sleep and Relaxation:

Sleep is essential for reducing stress for a number of reasons.

The body may heal its organs, muscles, and tissues while you sleep. The brain integrates and consolidates information from the day when we sleep, and this physical restoration is crucial for preserving general health and stress tolerance. It also aids in cognitive regeneration. This enhances one's capacity for learning, memory, and decision-making.

Getting enough sleep aids in controlling the hormonal shifts that lead to the synthesis of stress hormones such as cortisol. Stress, anxiety, and other hormones like melatonin and serotonin which are essential for mood stabilization and relaxation can all be exacerbated by elevated cortisol levels.

Insufficient sleep is insufficient to maintain emotional stability, such as mood management. Anger, mood swings, and mental instability brought on by sleep deprivation can make it more difficult to handle stress. The brain processes emotional events during REM (Rapid Eye Movement) sleep, which is when good sleep promotes emotional resilience, a happy mood, and emotional processing. This aids people in comprehending and controlling their emotional responses to stress.

Insufficient sleep negatively affects cognitive function, attention span, and concentration, making it more difficult to deal with pressures. Those who get enough sleep are more creative and have greater problem-solving abilities, which helps them come up with better solutions in difficult times.It strengthens the immune system, assisting the body in warding off ailments and lessening the physical toll of stress and Chronic illnesses including obesity, diabetes, and heart disease are associated with poor sleep, which can raise stress levels overall.Positive coping strategies like mindfulness and relaxation techniques are more common among well-rested people than bad ones like substance usage.

It encourages brain plasticity, the brain's capacity to change in response to new knowledge and experiences. Being flexible is essential for reducing stress and building resilience.

Useful Advice for Increasing Sleep:

Establish a schedule, such as waking up and going to bed at the same time every day. Before heading to bed, engage in some warm bathing or read a book. Select a cool, quiet, and dark location. In addition to reducing screen time before bed and avoiding blue lighting in the evening, try to avoid alcohol, caffeine, and large meals just before bed.

Organization and Time Management:

Effective time management techniques are essential for reaching personal and professional goals, reducing stress, and boosting productivity. Here are some well-known and effective time management techniques: Prioritize tasks by using the Urgent and Important, Important but Not Urgent, Urgent but Not Important, and Neither Urgent Nor Important categories; focus on critical tasks to ensure long-term success; divide tasks into three categories using the segregate capital method: A (must-do), B (should-do), and C (nice-to-do). Complete assignments A, B, and C in that order.

Planning and Scheduling:

Make a list of everything you need to get done and write it down. To maintain organization, update the list frequently and set aside designated times for various jobs or activities. This makes sure that significant jobs have time to be focused on.As you schedule time each day and each week to plan your activities and assess your success, make another list for weekly planning.Make a fresh timetable in accordance with your needs if you are uncomfortable or unable to stick to your timetables due to outside employment.

SMART goal-setting can help you achieve your objectives by ensuring that they are clear, quantifiable, doable, timely, and realistic. The SMART technique encourages you to work harder, provides you with direction, and aids in goal organization and achievement. To make your goals more reachable and traceable, clearly describe them.

After working for 25 to 30 minutes, take a 5-minute rest.After four intervals, take a long break of 20 to 30 minutes and spend that time doing something enjoyable, like spending time with loved ones or enjoying music. This will help you stay mentally refreshed, focus better, and avoid burnout. However, always remember to return to your task.If the activity is group-based, finish it all at once to reduce cognitive burden and boost productivity. When feasible, delegate work to others. This will free up your time so you may concentrate on more important things.To make bigger activities more manageable most of the time, divide them into smaller ones.If a task takes less than five minutes, finish it right away so you may feel accomplished. If you put it off until later, you could feel too sluggish or exhausted to finish it. Utilize technology, such as digital calendars or other apps, to remind yourself to do tasks before the due date. This way, you'll be reminded ahead of time. You should also routinely assess your progress and pinpoint areas that require improvement in order for you to perform better the next time.

You may improve productivity, lower stress levels, and strike a better work-life balance by implementing these time management strategies into your everyday routine.

Developing Resilience:

It takes a combination of mental, physical, and emotional techniques to build resilience against stress. Prior to taking on obstacles, mentally prepare yourself by rearranging your cognitive abilities and altering your negative thought patterns.Learn to recognize illogical thoughts and swap them out for sensible, upbeat ones.Imagine accomplishments and favorable results. This can help with drive and self-assurance as well as emotional development, such as forging close bonds with friends and family. Having a solid support network may be reassuring and beneficial when things go tough.Recognize your feelings and what causes them. This self-awareness can aid in controlling stress-related reactions.Don't hold your emotions within. To express your feelings, write in a notebook or speak with a trusted person.

Take part in enjoyable and soothing activities for yourself. Engaging in hobbies can be a beneficial way to decompress. A few pastimes that can help you decompress include playing with pets, drawing, cooking, watching movies, reading books, and taking walks in a serene area while the breeze is cool.If you enjoy traveling, taking trips and visiting beaches will also help you feel refreshed. Using a stress ball can occasionally also make you feel less stressed.Engaging in volunteer labor or community activities. Assisting others can help lower stress and give one a feeling of purpose. Be flexible as things change. Gaining adaptability in how you tackle issues will make it easier for you to handle unforeseen pressures. Think back on the past and draw lessons from it.

Gaining insight from your past stress management experiences can help you deal with the stress you face now.Participate in spiritual or religious activities occasionally if you find them meaningful. These may bring solace and tranquility.Practice thankfulness on a regular basis. Your general well-being and stress levels might be raised by concentrating on your blessings. Combining these techniques can help you become more resilient to stress, which will raise your general well-being and quality of life.

CONCLUSION:

Although stress is a normal reaction to difficult or demanding circumstances, prolonged stress can have detrimental effects on one's physical and mental well-being. It's critical to recognize stressors and establish healthy coping strategies, such as exercise, mindfulness, and constructive social connections. Obtaining expert assistance when required is also essential to successfully managing stress. Early stress recognition and management can improve general well being and promote a more balanced lifestyle.

Since most people, from children to adults, experience excessive stress, those who do so can seek therapy from therapists or enroll in therapy programs.If they are alcoholics, they can attempt to gradually cut back by speaking with pharmacologists.Stress is a big problem for both people and businesses. Prolonged stress leads to exhaustion. There are numerous strategies that people and organizations can employ to mitigate the detrimental effects of excessive stress on their health and performance at work. Organizational existence involves emotions. It is easier for people to control their emotions when they understand them. While emotional intelligence may assist people in managing the emotional demands of their professions, emotional labor itself may be very draining on individuals.

If you have a ton of ideas racing through your mind and are feeling anxious, you may actually get clarity in life and process your thoughts with the aid of just one habit. I've been doing it for a couple of years, and I owe it everything—including my mental tranquility. The practice I'm referring to is journaling, which is essentially recording your emotions to get insight into your inner world. However, I understand that many of you are unsure of where to begin, so I have a suggestion for you with an example: What have you given up on in life? Simply write down your own questions and respond to at least one of them each day to gain a great deal more self-awareness.

My advice to the public is to take preventative measures to lead a wave-less life,without stress. Everyone has stress in their lives, as we all know, but you have to handle it patiently, show society that you are resilient, and set a positive example for those who end their lives due to demands in their lives at a young age? Though life is brief, make a good reputation for in society by being brave and by never being a bad or negative person in the eyes of others.Stress is a natural part of life, it can be managed by using the methods mentioned in this book to lead a stress free existence.

Reference

Rein-hart, T. (2004). **The processing cost of reference set computation: Acquisition of stress shift and focus.** Language Acquisition, 12(2), 109-155.

Zapf, D., Dormann, C., & Frese, M. (1996). **Longitudinal studies in organizational stress research: a review of the literature with reference to methodological issues. Journal of occupational health psychology, 1(2), 145.**

Jayashree, R. (2010). **Stress management with special reference to public sector bank employees in Chennai.** International Journal of Enterprise and Innovation Management Studies, 1(3), 34-35.

Maratsos, M. P. (1973). **The effects of stress on the understanding of pronominal co-reference in children.** Journal of Psycholinguistic Research, 2, 1-8.